Boring Sports…..……………………..……………..3
> *Hunting*
> *Baseball*

Other stuff……………………………..…………........12
> *Waiting in Lines*
> *What Happened to Pluto?*
> *Homelessness*
> *H-Mart*
> *I identify three causes of my poor health and rapid heartbeat, then propose an irrelevant solution*
> *Babies are Overrated*
> *Diversity in the USA*
> *Leave Buffalo*
> *Getting a Job*
> *The Snooze Button*
> *Insurance*
> *Getting Accepted Into School*
> *Kids*

Animals………………………………………….……46
> *Cows*
> *Dogs*
> *Gorillas*
> *Squirrels*
> *Skunks*

Boring Sports

Hunting

Men hunt because it's the last socially acceptable activity available that allows them to both get away from their wife and kill something at the same time, other than said wife. Another popular reason guys say they hunt is "I dunno, just cuz." I'm not saying people shouldn't hunt, I'm just saying that it's a stupid waste of time.

A lot of people say they hunt for food, not realizing that food isn't something you hunt, it's something you buy at a grocery store. If food was something that needed to be hunted, then one could say that I go hunting all the time, even during the off-season. Indeed, I did go on one hunting trip when I was kid with my friend Mike, which I considered to be pretty successful, though the owner of the bird-feeder seemed to think otherwise. Nevertheless, the bird incident, and I'm not going to spell it out for you – just know that it was bad, was enough inspiration for me to spend the remainder of my life not killing for sport, and I'm thankful for the many hours of my life this has saved me. My purpose for writing then, is to offer up a few pointers (eight to twelve to be exact, and to make it worthwhile) that you may wish to consider if you have not already when you go hunting for yourself.

First, I start by hunting for a good coupon. Mom says that $1.99 for a pound of chicken breast is pretty good, so that's a good starting point. Once I decide what I want which, in this case is chicken, I start thinking about where I'll go. I search for the supermarket with the biggest rack –

clearance rack, that is (aka manager special), and then I get into my car and drive there. I know it doesn't sound exotic so in order to spice it up, I listen to the same CD repeatedly on high volume, and it keeps me entertained. You might even say that it's more interesting than staring at a tree for nine hours, which is what happens when you go hunting in the woods.

Once I choose the appropriate venue, which usually happens to be the supermarket closest to where I live, I go there and circle the aisles, methodically stalking my prey, which almost always can be found in a cooler at the back of the store next to the lobsters. Once I find what I'm looking for which, in this case is chicken drumsticks, and have it literally in the palm of my hands, I pull the trigger by tossing it into my cart before proceeding to the nearest cash register where I'm greeted by a nice young man and/or woman who is waiting to ask me if I found everything okay. Sometimes before I proceed to the checkout I stare at the lobster tank and think to myself what a sick man the butcher is for allowing this blatant charade of animal cruelty to continue without question. When I stare at him he just smiles and says hello, and I move on without incident. At the register, they scan my shit, and if one of the items is too big and doesn't fit in a bag or if it's a candy bar or something that I want to eat right away, it gets tagged with a "PAID" sticker. Unlike the woods, there is no limit to the number of items you can have tagged at the supermarket, which is another perk to hunting in the 21st century.

One of my favorite things to hunt in the supermarket is bacon. It's delicious, and you can do a lot of things with it, like put it in a bacon stretcher or on a sandwich. I don't know what a bacon stretcher is or does. It sounds kind of dumb, and all of these bacon-related activities result in the same grizzly fate for the bacon, which is my consuming it, so I wonder if all the bacon-related accessories are necessary, or if I can just bypass it all and proceed directly to eating the bacon and then move on with my life. I guess some things in this world aren't questioning, and this is definitely one of them.

You thought I was done with bacon? Nope, there's more. Bacon is a relatively easy item to hunt, but there are some variations, usually having to do with how much sodium is in it. For purposes of your hunt, you'll want avoid low-sodium or reduced sodium because it takes away from the deliciousness of the bacon, and your taste buds are more important than your heart anyway. This isn't the only obstacle you'll be faced when buying your meat. Another common challenge you'll encounter in the bacon aisle is which brand to buy. The most effective way to resolve this issue is to locate the most expensive brand, then shift your eyes a little and find the off-brand version next to that and just get that one. You'll save a few bucks, and feel good about yourself because you shopped smart. You can donate those extra dollars to the Salvation Army guy jingling his bell on the way out, or to the next person who asks you for free money in exchange for nothing, which will happen three to four times before you even make it to your m-f'ing car.

Finally, be very careful when hunting for bacon because the anti-bacon hipster movements, which are a coalition faction of feminists and liberals, are now peddling turkey bacon, which is delicious in its own right, but should not be confused at all with actual bacon, and this is a source of considerable controversy in the bacon-consumption community. Speaking of stretch, other bacon-related controversies include whether or not two slabs of bacon of the same sex who love each other, should be allowed to marry. Same-sex bacon marriage supporters don't perceive this as a two-sided argument, whereas the right-flank nutjobs are too ignorant and old to understand anything, much less the concept of love, but these two groups actually make up a very small minority of the entire population, who, according to every poll ever administered, couldn't care less either way, and wish everyone would just shut up or start talking about ways to save the ice caps. I'm definitely in that third category.

     Another fun animal to hunt is the cow. There are so many varieties of beef in the store: sirloin, ribs, rump, rib eye, t-bone, ground, prime rib, NY strip, thin rib, flank, and they're all delicious, and vary in price. You'll have to do some research yourself on the different kinds of beef, but once you narrow it down, hunting for the perfect piece can be a challenge, but there is a proven of method of selecting the best piece of meat in the store. The way I do it is to stand there for a while and watch someone methodically pick up the hunks of meat, inspect them, put them down, until they find the two best pieces, at which point they will select the best one, and leave the second best one. That's when I swoop in and snatch that second one up. This method for choosing the best slab is time-consuming, as some losers will stand there for literally twenty minutes deciding which piece to get before choosing, so you'll have to wait it out. Sometimes, these people end up choosing no piece at all, which is beyond dumb. Always remember though, when using this hunting technique, that there is no shame in second best, and don't worry about how they knew which piece of meat was better – if you want to spend your life honing the craft of picking out meat in the supermarket, go ahead; I'm going to spend mine not doing that.

Other animals, like the turkey, are easier to hunt. When hunting for turkey, it's important to remember that the turkey is more scared of you than you are of it, and usually it's frozen – so be careful not to drop it on your foot, which can cause complications later in the day when you want to put your shoe back on. Like hunting deer in the woods, size matters when it comes to picking out a turkey. You want the biggest bird you can find or, if your family is small, the smallest one. If you're a family of one, they sell a great little rotisserie bird at walmart for $5. Actually, I think it's a chicken, but who cares as long it's moist and hot. Plus, it's cost effective. If you are going to go the little bird route, you may want to reexamine your life and look into getting yourself a family. The great thing about families is that if you don't have one, you can just create your own, and this way you can buy a bigger, more interesting bird. If you are in the market for a bigger turkey, you should always make sure it says "butterball" on it. Butterball is the Kleenex of turkeys. I don't know why, I've just got a good feeling about butterball, and the blue and yellow color scheme resonates, but I'm not here to talk about marketing, I'm here to talk about hunting. Well, I'm not actually here or talking, but you get the point.

While the hunt for the perfect turkey is important, the real work is in its presentation. The difference between a good and bad turkey is its level of moistness, and it needs to be very moist. If the turkey comes out dry, it's not a big deal – all you need to do is throw it in the garbage and cook a new one, or lubricate it with some turkey rub or something. If you want to know what makes the turkey so moist, I have no idea – you'll want to ask the woman who cooked it, she'll probably have a clue. Cooking is one of those rare things in life about which the fairer sex can speak intelligently, and the best time to approach her is after everyone is done eating and she is working through the dishes, the reason being that it's a relatively mindless activity and she can focus all of her attention on your stupid questions. One thing I do know about cooking these things from having watched enough times is that if you've never had your arm elbow-deep into a giant bird's ass, but want to, then this a great opportunity for you. Nobody knows why the store puts the giblets back in bird after they've already detached and removed them, but they do. While I may not know how to cook the bird tastily, I do know how to eat it and am happy to advise a little bit on the subject, which I'll do in the next paragraph.

By the time the turkey gets to you, it's already cooked and sliced, so all you have to do is reach onto the plate with your fork, pick the one you like the most, and put it on your plate. It sounds simple, I know, but you'd be surprised. Take some time and think about it, but always try to be the first one to choose to ensure that you, and not some other jerk in the family, get the best piece. The most difficult part of this process is choosing between white and dark meat; I generally go for the white meat, but what makes hunting fun is one's individual preference.

Baseball

Baseball is a great game to play if you love standing around and doing nothing for long periods of time. The games are literally endless, which is a shame because whenever I am watching a baseball game, the part I look most forward to is the end.

If you're a baseball player, the requirements for making it in the big leagues are basically non-existent, unless you're the pitcher or are exceptionally good at batting. Some people have disagreed by arguing that the most important position in the sport is either first base or short-stop. Obviously these people are wrong, because baseball is not a sport. (note: neither is golf).

If you're the pitcher, baseball is great, because your job is to throw a ball as hard as you can at someone else, which is awesome. If you hit him, all he gets is a free trip to first base and so there's no real incentive to aim anywhere except at his head or knee cap. With the only punishment being a free base, and the occasional charging of the mound, it is difficult to pass up the opportunity to clip a dude on the other team in the back with a 90 mph fastball. This is assuming you're good at pitching; for me it'd be more like 35mph and there's a high probability I would miss. That's okay though – "dust yourself off and try again." If, for some reason, the hitter does choose to charge the mound, it's best to just run away like a baby and let your teammates handle it, or throw some more fastballs at him while he's running towards you in hopes that you're able to peg him in the head and knock him to the ground or, ideally, unconscious – the latter is known as a "home run." If you're really good pitching, you could try and break every batter's arm by hitting them in the elbow, which is good strategy because you would win by default since everyone on the opposing team would be injured ©. I'm copywriting this idea that because I bet baseball analysts and players have never thought doing that, and so when they do, I want to get a check.

If you're not the pitcher, baseball is a lot of standing around in the field doing nothing if you enjoy doing that and getting paid a billion dollars an hour, or grew up in a field on a farm, you might consider trying out for your local team. Another reason people play baseball is to have their chance to hit the ball, which occurs once every three hours or so. Batting gives you an opportunity to get revenge on the pitcher by hitting it directly back at him. The odds of you hitting the pitcher are much lower than the odds of the pitcher hitting you, but if you do succeed at getting him with a "come-backer," the payout is huge since the velocity at which the ball would be travelling when you connect it would significantly greater than when it's coming at you, and could therefore do a lot more damage to him. There's a good chance that if you do it just right you will kill him, which in baseball is known as a "grand slam." Another good thing about batting is that it afford kids an opportunity to learn about taking turns, which will come in handy as an adult, for instance, while driving in rush hour traffic. Studies* show that baseball players, because of their ability to occupy long periods of time doing nothing while waiting their turn, become great drivers. So, next time you see someone driving like an asshole, you can almost guarantee that they weren't a baseball player. *No studies show that, I just made it up.

Another great thing about baseball is when the coaches get into a fight with the umpire. These hissy fits, which are actually quite sexual in nature, never get old. I could watch them all day and be surprised by the outcome every time, despite the fact they always end the same – with the umpire kicking the coach out and the coach storming off the field. Before retreating, the mad coach grabs a bag and throws it and kicks a little sand, before exiting the stadium and bursting into tears.

The fight starts with a slow steady build up where the coaches disagree with a call the umpire made, and this prompts him to approach the umpire him on the field, shouting and waving his hands like an ape, until their lips are nearly touching. They continue yelling at each other at the same time and getting angrier and angrier until the climax, which finally occurs when the umpire lifts up his mask and says the line "you're outta here!" He must say "you're outta here" or it doesn't count, and this is simple baseball fight protocol.

Every time I watch one of these fights it gets me riled up, and I envision myself doing the same thing, usually in the grocery store or something. I imagine being at the checkout at the grocery store up in the cashier's face over the price of an item or whether or not I have too many things for the 12 item limit at the express checkout, at which point store manager would come over and be like "you're outta here!" Then I would walk out of the store, dropping a bag of oranges on the ground for me to kick, then throw some of my cold cuts across before exiting to cheering storegoers. Actually, when you think about it, these fights are lame. I wish they were more like hockey fights… Come to think of it hockey fights are lame too, I wish those fights were more like MMA fights, except instead of having tapouts there were no tapouts and it was guaranteed there would be a death or you get your money back. Now that's old school.

Other Stuff

Waiting in Lines
"33% of your life is spent working, 33% sleeping, 10% of your life getting ready work, and the remaining 24% waiting in lines" - a statistic I just made up

I'm amazed every time I see a line, mostly because of peoples' determination to wait in them, mine included. Everyone in the line is standing there thinking the same thing, that everyone else should die or leave so they can mail their package and go home. Instead, we wait in mutual disgust not saying anything or making eye contact for what is often an unbearable amount of time.

I'm so conditioned to stand in lines that, if I see a bunch of people that even look like they're in a line, I'll jump right behind them, even if it's not the line I'm supposed to be in. This happens in traffic a lot. The left lane will be empty and I get tempted to pass all the cars who are lined up in the right lane in order to get further ahead, but I know that I'll have to merge eventually so to avoid the inevitable confrontation and being 'that guy', I just get behind everyone else. Usually I don't know where I'm going, so I wind up sitting in a lot of lines I don't need to be in.

One thing that causes lines on the roadways is tolls. Tolls confuse me for a lot of reasons, the biggest of which being that I thought the government used the 40% of wages it takes from people when they get paid to pave the roads. I guess not, and so sometimes you need to pull over and hand over more money, which makes traffic go even slower. The only good part about this is that it conserves your brakes because when you're stuck in traffic as a result of the traffic jams toll booths cause, you don't need to slam on them to slow down and pay the toll. To make things more confusing on the road, politicians are now making it illegal to avoid these tolls. They call it back tracking, and it's where you come up with creative ways to not pay the toll, and now it's illegal. Your toll, therefore, for not paying the toll, becomes a bigger toll…

      The problem with being accustomed to waiting in lines, aside from the fact it prevents you from living a healthy and happy life, is that it desensitizes you to the concept of not waiting in lines, which can be dangerous if you ever need to get anywhere. Moving to the front of a line can be a liberating and fulfilling life experience but usually when I have the opportunity to skip the line, I have no idea what to do because it's such a foreign concept, and so I usually hop back in line because change is scary. Unless it's change I can believe in, which usually isn't the case.   Standing in line isn't always bad, and you actually see a lot of good deeds being done in them. Sometimes, when I feel like being nice, I'll let the person behind me with less groceries go ahead, or let the old lady driving next to me merge into my lane. Good deeds in line make me feel better about me, and it makes me happier this way than to donate money to charity, that's for sure, because it doesn't involve me giving anyone money in exchange for nothing, and if I all I'm conceding is my spot in line, that will only make me more patient for the next time I inevitably have to stand in a long, stupid line.

One day, I decided I didn't feel like waiting in line anymore and so I got these VIP concert tickets that allowed me to walk right past the general public line (cough cough losers cough ahem excuse me) waiting to get in the venue. It was definitely one of the longer lines I have ever seen – probably a good quarter mile long, and so it felt pretty good to just walk right by them. I didn't make eye contact because I didn't want to hurt their feelings or make them jealous, but secretly it was the greatest feeling I have ever known – which probably says a lot about my life. It was great because not only did I not have to wait in line, but for those 30 seconds I was better than everyone else in the room, and that's what really counts. It was both a liberating and scary experience to bypass the entire line and proceed straight to the front of it, and I'm a better person because of it. "What doesn't kill you makes you stronger," right? Except, of course, what kills you.

Since that experience, whenever I want to feel better about myself I just go to where there is a big line and walk past everyone. Likewise, if things are going a little too well (i.e. I'm not waiting in a line), and I need to find that balance, I go find me a long line to stand in and it makes everything feel like normal. When I'm looking for a good line to stand in, I usually go to Starbucks. They have the best and longest lines in the morning, which is stupid really, because you'd think they would have figured out by now that 8 am is their busy hour. Most days, when I go to Starbucks and see the line I just keep driving because I don't have time to get out of the traffic line to get into the coffee line to get back into the traffic line. I wish I was joking...

What Happened to Pluto?

Pluto is still a planet. Just because you erase something from a diagram or picture doesn't mean it doesn't exist anymore. To prove this point, consider that I once went to my dad's house and there was a wooden diagram with a little stick figure representing each member of the family, and I wasn't one of them. Although I wasn't necessarily around, I was still out there floating in space, and so to correct this injustice, I scribbled in a stick figure drawing of myself and sent them an updated photo of me slumped over in the corner at some rave party wearing an awesome hat. What made the hat awesome is that I purchased it at the grocery store for a cool six dollars. It was camouflage and had ear flaps and lots of fake fur on the inside. Side note: I'm wearing the hat right now, and it's still awesome.

As you can see in the image to the left, there is a black spot in the space where Pluto used to be. It wasn't until I dug a little deeper in the exhibit that I found traces of the poor planet sitting alone on bookshelf next to a book of the other eight planets. While it was sad to know that Pluto had to embark on his own struggle, it was good to see that he ended up getting his own spot on the front of the book, while the others had to share one book. In this way, Pluto had succeeded in becoming relevant despite the odds being stacked against him, and the other planets resented Pluto for that, and were even jealous that he had made name for himself. This confused Pluto and bothered him, but he went on living his life, and so did the others, except they had to work every day while he spent most of his time in the hot tub with beautiful comets because he didn't have to share his book royalties eight different ways.

One of the reasons Pluto was put into the special needs class, if I recall correctly, was because he couldn't keep up with the rest of the planets; for instance, it would take longer for Pluto than the others to rotate around the sun, and his path would cross with the others, which somehow made him less of a planet. Compare it to getting lapped in a race. In fact, if Pluto were a race car driver, he would definitely be Danica Patrick, mostly because it's small, can't drive, and is always a few laps behind everyone else. I'm just kidding of course; if Pluto was any more like Danica Patrick, we'd have died a long time ago because it would have crashed right into Earth like it was a wall in Daytona.

Pluto disappeared from existence some five years ago, probably due to budget cuts and the recession of 2008. Pluto, as is widely known, was the most boring planet in the solar system, mostly because it was the smallest and furthest away from the sun, but I don't think this means it needed to be deleted. The only thing I really know about Pluto is that it used to be a planet, and now it isn't, and that this apparently occurred with little to no protest from anyone; one day I woke up and Pluto wasn't a planet anymore, and if I did happen to know what day that was, I'd be a bigger loser than the little planet that couldn't. If any planet should have been erased from the map of the universe, it's Mercury. Mercury is that one planet I always forget about when listing the planets, and in this regard, is way more of a nuisance than Pluto was.

Upon reflection, I'm not sure we need to get rid of any planets. If you're trying to attract people to careers in astronomy, it would make more sense to add planets instead. If you keep getting rid of them, there would be nothing to study. The first planet I propose that we add is the Moon, because we can see it, and some people have been to it. How awesome is that? Also, we wouldn't have to explain to people what a moon is when they ask; we could just call it a planet and leave it at that, which is an ideal situation. By the way, what is a moon? Sure the moon might not really be a planet, but an honorary degree isn't an actual degree, and we still give those out. At the least, the moon should be an honorary planet. Besides, the moon is the only cool thing in the sky aside from the sun that we can see, and deserves planetary status. Is the sun a planet? I don't know, I just don't. The reality of all this planet controversy, however, is that the only planet worth knowing is Earth. It's the best for many reasons, most notably its beautiful beaches, epic mountain ranges, and gorgeous women.

Homelessness

Big cities are made up of essentially two things: rats and homeless people. As someone who grew up with a pet rat, I know that they get hungry. At the same time, homeless people, or if you want to be politically correct, "people without homes" need to go somewhere. By feeding the homeless to the rats, you'd be solving the problem of hungry rats and homelessness at the same time, a real win-win IMO.

Now before you think I am being insensitive to the dietary needs of rats, please bear in mind that the rats are starving and malnourished, and this would at least cover their most basic needs. For that reason, we would need to supplement the bum meat with essential vitamins and minerals, namely, fish oil and Vitamin D. Fish oil because it promotes a soft, shiny coat, which rats appreciate, and vitamin D because rats spend most of their time foraging at night in the garbage can and therefore miss out on the essential nutrients that the sun provides.

The H-Mart

The H-mart is a fun supermarket. It's an Asian supermarket chain, and carries a lot of bizarre Asian products. Seaweed, live crabs, cat bbq, and random Korean treats. On weekends, you can get a ton of free samples and, twice a year, free samples of the popular Asian rice wine, sake. Don't ask me how or why it's legal to serve free alcohol in the store. The Asians play by a different set of rules, probably because they own us, and you know what? I get it.

The difficult part about shopping at the H-mart is that it's got a bunch of stuff that you normally don't see anywhere else and so you get strong impulses to buy a bunch of it because you fear you won't get another chance to. It's one of those places where you don't want to let your eye wander too much because you might run out for some toilet paper and come back with a live squid and try to keep it as a pet.

The other day my roommate went to the H-mart for some paper towels and came home with one of those must-have items that you don't see anywhere else. He bursted through the door, brimming with joy. "Look what I found at the H-mart..." he said, holding a huge bag of unboiled peanuts. My first thought/question to myself was "Peanuts need to be boiled?" and my second thought was, "Why do you need that?" and my final thought was "actually yeah that is a pretty good find. Nice work..." And then he boiled the peanuts and we ate peanuts for dinner three days in a row.

I identify three causes of my poor health and rapid heartbeat, then propose an irrelevant solution:
Cause #1, Taco Bell

I get diarrhea thinking about Taco Bell. At one point, they said that Taco Bell meat wasn't even officially meat, yet people continue to eat there. I was devastated when I heard that the meat at Taco Bell was made of cat shards or something, and not due to the harm the ingredients were causing to my body, but because there was a real possibility that Taco Bell would go out of business and I wouldn't be able to get any more tacos. They already took the #14 chicken / taco combo away from me, and now this?

I can accept some public safety laws, like seatbelts, but to know there are forces out there right now threatening to take away my ability to eat grease-soaked horse giblets stuffed into a delicious shell... well, blame Canada. Lucky for me, big corporations and CEO's don't have to abide by the same laws as normal people, and the chain not only stayed open, but everyone got a huge raise and Christmas bonus except anyone who wasn't a CEO.

#2, Chipotle

Chipotle should fire everyone, then turn the sneeze guard around so customers can scoop their own food. It would be easier for me to portion out my own white or brown rice, black or pinto beans, choose between chicken, steak, and whatever carnitas is, throw some green peppers and onions on there without having to ask for them because for some reason its employees skip right over them like

they're not even there, and top it off with some pico de guy-o, hot sauce, cheese and lettuce, and leave without being upsold for a drink and chips*. By doing this, Chipotle execs could pocket 7$ more an hour that may have wound up in the paycheck of one of its slaves, I mean employees.
*seriously, get the chips

#3, Subway

It's getting to the point where I have to train the employees Subway on how to do their job. Usually the bread is stale and so I first have to ask them to bake a new one. Then, since I'm accustomed to the menu, if there's a new employee and they have to look on the sandwich board for directions, I end up telling them what goes on the thing in order to save us both time and me the humiliation of me pointing with my index finger and grunting like a monkey while another grown man or woman attempts to decipher the message.

For being sandwich artists, they must be more into abstract art, because often, I am handed an assortment of random shit rolled up in wax paper and shoved into a bag with some napkins, and it's left up to my imagination to envision the contents of the bag as a sandwich. When this occurs, I am forced to either train the employee myself or accept something that resembles a Paul Walker crash scene, and since I came for a sandwich, I generally opt for the the former. If it weren't for Subway's great deals, I would probable say something (OK not really), but when you consider specials like FebruANY, where all of the sandwiches are $5, Subtember (who cares what the special is, that's a great name), and my personal favorite, the $2 cold cut combo 6 inch (this one is happening now), it's difficult to stay mad at them for long.

     One solution I have to solve almost all of these problems is whenever I go to a fast food chain, I scoop my own "food" or deep-fry my own ash nuggets while they help me mail my packages and letters. This is an ideal situation for me because I hate mailing letters more than just about anything in the world. Not because I don't want people to get mail from me, but because it's a nightmare of a process. When I think about it about what it takes to mail a letter or package, I break down and cry. For instance, you need to know how big of a package you can stick into the blue thing, you need to know how much postage you have to put on it, where to get the postage, whether or not the post office is open and where the post office is, what time the post office closes for lunch, and you need to make a point to make a scene at the post-office while standing in line there for the better part of the afternoon so that everyone knows you hate the post office. But it's not done there. You need to have the address of the person to whom you're going to mail the thing and if you don't, the phone number. When you call, you'll need to explain to them why you're asking them for their address again even though they gave you it last week because you don't have an address book, and they'll ask you why you don't have one and then advise you to get one and you'll say okay I'll get one but really be thinking just shut up and and tell me your address, not to mention the inevitable small talk and pleasantries that must take place during phone calls. There's more. You'll need to know where the blue thing is that you need to drop the package, and actually remember to mail it which is a huge pain in the ass plus you have to drive to wherever the blue box is, and then if you do forget to mail it, you'll be constantly reminded of what a failure you are for not doing so when you get in your car every day and see it there on the backseat, and if it's a check, you might never be able to buy a house because now you'll have bad credit. So, for all these reasons, if fast-food restaurants focused more on helping me mail my letters, I wouldn't be so upset about putting 7,000 calories of food-substitute into my stomach - not that it matters to either way to them because the only thing I'm really going to do about it anyway is continue to eat there. But if this were a possibility, the corporations would benefit too because they can continue making profit by feeding us bone marrow because I would be so thrilled that someone helped me mail a package, and so it would be a win-win.

Babies are Overrated

No other person in the world can go through life doing the things babies do and get away with it. Babies are boring, can't do anything for themselves, have receding hairlines, are chubby, but everyone loves them. Babies can't even sit up straight, which is ridiculous. Sitting a baby down is like stacking wood. If you don't do it just right, it falls over and you have to pick it up and balance it perfectly so it doesn't fall over again. If it does have trouble staying upright, you can just wedge some more pieces of wood against it so it stays put. As a tiny person, it must be frustrating to be flopped over on your side on the couch crying in a puddle of your own urine and drool because you couldn't hold your breast milk. If a big person were to do that, it would be so embarrassing, and they would probably feel dumb. They would go to work the next day and explain how it got a little off balance on the couch and tipped over, and remained in that position motionless until someone picked it back up. Telling stories like that is definitely not how friends are won, and so the baby would probably be a loser and bullied and wind up taking a gun to school.

Babies do tons of awful things and nobody seems to mind – like pooping their pants every twenty minutes and throwing up on everything. For babies, not only are these things tolerable, sometimes people think it's cute when, in reality, they should be left in the corner until they're old enough to stack wood.

At Thanksgiving one time, a new baby in the family was sitting in the middle of the living room drinking milk or something from a baby bottle, and everyone was just standing around watching him. It took the baby like twenty minutes to finish all the milk and when it did, everyone said "aww" and then the baby threw up all over the place and they kept thinking it was cute. I was so irritated and so to prove I could outdrink the baby I picked up a bottle, of beer, and asked everyone to watch as I slammed it down in about three seconds, then threw up all over the place. Not only did everyone keep paying attention only to the baby, but they also told me to leave. I thought that was pretty unfair so I threw a temper tantrum like a baby. Nobody thought that was cute either.

One good thing about babies is that they're a great way to get positive attention from women. Well, as positive attention as you can hope for from a guy willing to use a small person as date bait. If you're a guy and want to meet girls, a great way to do it is by borrowing someone else's baby and taking it out in public. It doesn't really matter where, but chicks will flock to you like pigeons to bread. They'll want to know if the baby is yours, but so that you don't have to explain to them where the baby is on your first date, you can tell them that it's your sister's baby and that you were babysitting. They'll think you're a great uncle and would make a great dad one day, and will find you irresistible. If you end up going on a few dates with the girl and they become persistent on seeing the baby again you can tell them it died from natural causes, or get another baby from somewhere because they all pretty much look the same and have that distinctive new baby smell.

When using babies to flirt with ladies, be sure not to use a baby carrier. This will communicate non-verbally with the woman how tough you are, and a baby carrier would make you look weak – kind of like carrying around a purse, and men rarely carry around purses. If at all possible, carry the baby around upside down by its feet so both the baby and the woman knows who the boss is.

It is important to mention that this does not mean that the baby cannot serve some of the same functions as the purse. Say, for instance, you get attacked by someone who wants to steal your wallet. If this happens and you're carrying a baby, you can use the baby like a purse and hit the thief over the head with it – making sure that you are striking the perpetrator with the baby's head because at that age, it's the hardest part on the body. I would suggest using this as a last resort because, although others will forgive you because you sacrificed the well-being of the baby to save your own life, you may suffer crippling emotional devastation from having injured the child in the process.

There are some instances where having a baby makes sense, the main one being that you can always use him or her as an excuse to be late to work, or not go in at all. If your baby is sick, or even if it isn't, you can just say the word baby to your boss or teacher, and you don't have to go to work. The only other acceptable reason to miss work is if a relative dies, but even that's becoming taboo anymore, and so babies are the wave of the future. An older friend of mine's grandmother passed away; she was 98 years old and he is fifty. He was talking about going away to help with her funeral and see family, and so I asked him what he told his employer because if he told them that his grandma died and so he had to go take off work they would never believe it because he was pretty old himself. I suggested that instead, he should say that his baby needed its rabies shots, and he took my advice and his work gave him a paid vacation and a trip to Disney World! This is obviously one of those rare instances where having a baby would be sensible.

Diversity in the USA (one of each colour)

America is a unique country, and is known for its ethno-diversity because since the founders made America in 1776, people from all over Mexico and El Salvadore have had the opportunity to come here to pursue their dream of cleaning hotel rooms and not learning English. Someone should probably them that it's better in Canada.

When there are three or more different colored people in one spot, it's called diversity. Think of it as laundry. There are whites, darks, and everything else – and the whites are always separate. When speaking about diverse groups of people, it's important never to refer to them by skin color or as "them people," unless they're white, and then it's fine to say whatever you want. This is because white folks have been trained to apologize for everything, and so are not allowed to get offended. Whites' apologetic nature is due to the awful things they have done to others throughout history, things that I am expected to take responsibility for as a white person, even though I wasn't around for any of them. Examples include slavery from the 1700's through the 1900's of African-Americans, and exploiting and driving native americans away from their land. Slavery, yeah that was pretty bad, and again, I'm sorry, but I wasn't there. Plus, there's nothing that can be done about it now anyway, unless these minority groups unite and want to do something crazy, like round up all the white people and kill them off in order to make a supreme race or something like that. I know it's a bit far-fetched, but I was always told that there's no such thing as a bad idea (Mein Kampf, 1948).

It's not only popular to make fun of white people, it's also fun. This is due mostly to the fact that white culture is so boring. I say "they" even though I'm white because it's okay to speak in the third person if you're white because it's what douche bags do, and most white people are d-bags. We are a boring, predictable people with a handful of redeeming qualities, like the ability to "hold down a job" and be President of the United States, and nothing we like is interesting. This mockery of our pale species is widespread; they name movies and books after us, like "white man can't jump" or the popular book "stuff white people like." I, for one, take offense to both of these titles, not because I'm actually offended, but because it's my job as an American to get offended by anything and everything. Being offended showcases my ignorance, and perpetuates my narcissism and sense of self-importance which is what I need in order to compensate for not being important to anyone except my mom, who by law of nature is obliged to care for me, unless she falls into that weird category of female who decides to dispose of their child in a garbage can, drown them in a tub, or shake them like a polaroid picture. Popular child killers include Casey Anthony (nutjob) and whoever killed Jon Benet Ramsey (I assume it was OJ…)

For these reasons, white people have developed a good sense of humor. Well, not really, but could you imagine a movie being made called "black people are great dancers" or "stuff black people like?" If you are someone who has some good ideas for what should go in either of these productions then congratulations, you're racist, and the last thing you want to be called is racist because they're the most discriminated against.

Did you know there are more than two races? Yes, it was news to me, but there are! Most Americans think that all Asian people are Chinese, and this couldn't be further from the truth. Yes, Asia is a big continent, or whatever it is, and is made up of multiple nations whose people look the same and have the same name (Kim), but it would be superficial to not see them for their inward differences – and there are many. I won't go into these differences in detail because I have no idea what they are, but I know the important ones. Actually, to my knowledge, there is only one, which is this: what we call "pets," people in China call "food." That's basically all there is to know about China.

Another emerging ethnogroup in the country is known as "people with disabilities." These people are evolving so quickly as a race that nobody knows what to call them. Oops, I violated the cardinal rule: don't refer to a group of people as a group of people... Confusing, I know, but it's 2014! Anyway, first came retard, then mentally challenged, then handicapped, then developmentally disabled, and now they're just individuals with disABILITIES. Nowhere is there mention of the absurdity of the dialogue that exists when these changes occur, but it is absurd and we should try bringing it up. Here, let me go first: your feeble attempt to define a group in order to secure your own comfort with their abnormal existence in your normal world is the real problem, and in this way, you are the one who suffers from a disability known as "not being able to not be a douche," and you may wish to contact a doctor. Your doctor can then prescribe you a healthy "cocktail" as they say in the disabled biz, which will likely consist of Risperdal, Seroquel, Klonopin,

Ritalin, Ativan, Depakote, Topamax, Calcium, and a sip of water.

Leave Buffalo

I'm not kidding when I tell you this place is a dump. If you think Buffalo is great, it means that you've never left it. Before I delve any further into the issue though, we need to define some terms. First, the word "city." A city is defined as a place that doesn't suck huge balls. Buffalo is, by definition, not a city. Okay, that's the only term we need to define at the moment. If any others arise I will let you know.

Do you know what Buffalo is famous for? If you answered "nothing," you were close. But the answer is Chicken Wings, terrible sports teams, and a place one drives through in order to get through Niagara Falls. And now food trucks I guess.

Let's talk about chicken wings first – or as they are known in other parts of the world where people date outside of their own family – "Buffalo wings." They cost seven cents to produce, yet we pay $7.00 for ten of them. The dumb part is that nobody asks why. And everyone has their favorite wing place, which is stupid because for they all look and taste delicious. To make these, you deep fry the wings the wings for 12 minutes, then dip them in sauce. The sauce is where you can get creative with wings. You can make them hot, medium, or mild by adding butter to it, and here is something I learned while working in the kitchen: add a little honey, and, to quote the butler from Scary Movie 2, "that just kicks it up a notch." Yum.

Second, terrible sports teams. Where do I begin. Dude misses a field goal 20 years ago, and PEOPLE STILL TALKING ABOUT IT. While you're sitting around crucifying Scott Norwood do you know what he's doing? Living the good life down South, not thinking about you for one second because you ran him out of town after giving him every hard earned dollar you ever made. Other major sports accomplishments include losing four straight super bowls, still having O.J. Simpson's name on a stadium, playing home football games in Canada, and giving Terell Owens the key to the city while he was in town for one losing season – well done.

Speaking of Canada: Niagara Falls. I love Niagara Falls as much as the next guy. But I think modern technology is ruining the splendor of this great wonder of the world. Like, unless Asians start wearing their smartphones around their neck instead of keeping them in their pocket, everything I love about Niagara Falls will be gone in a few years (which is Asians with cameras around their necks). It's weird, because every time I go to Niagara Falls, which is never, I always wish I went more, because it's so beautiful. But then I get home and realize that I am in Buffalo and when I wake up in the morning, still wishing I was in the Falls so I could try tightrope walking across the border...without a tether. I have no tightrope walking experience. You do the Math. You gotta give it to Nic Wallenda though, that was pretty awesome. I have no idea if he actually did pay his taxes afterwards, but I bet he was thrilled when he got to the Canadian side because he probably wanted to visit the butterfly conservatory and, of course, get just that much further away from Buffalo.

Finally, let's talk about food trucks. No, seriously, welcome to Buffalo, where there is conversation about food trucks. It's the dipping dots of restaurants. Don't worry though, we'll run them out of business too because it's what we do, probably by continuing to not pave the roads. Just ask the guys who were riding around on tricycles selling ice cream about the laws and crappy roads and whatnot.

There are plenty of great things to say about the region but I don't feel like it right now. I know this because I've spent much of my life living here, and could go on, but won't. To conclude, briefly, if you're not convinced by now that you should leave Buffalo…well, then, you must be from Buffalo, so let's Go Bills on three! 1.2…

Getting a Job

The first step towards finding a job is the interview. The first question of the interview is usually something along the lines of "so tell me about yourself," which isn't a question, but oh well. All they really want to hear about is what you did at your last job, so make sure you have a good story made up. If it's a true story, it probably won't get you anywhere. In fact, your best accomplishment at your last job may have very well involved taking a dump that was on par with that of the Guiness book of world records – mine sure was, but the interview is not the time to highlight that. You may even be so heartbroken by the fact that your record-breaking poop has gone unnoticed by your former employer that you feel the need to steal awards from other employees' desk and pass them off as your own in appreciation for your contributions to the company. Do it! It doesn't matter if you actually won the awards, it just matters that people think you did. Another thing you want to be conscious of throughout the interview process is your appearance. If you have a tattoo on your face, for instance, don't bother showing up – you're not getting the job. Also, go home and try scrubbing the tattoo off with a brillo pad. For applicants without a face tattoo, you want dress well, but you also want to make sure you're clean and don't smell like B.O. – which you probably do. Deodorant is a quick fix for that, and you can purchase deodorant at the store or request it from the clerk at any hotel lobby room. Also be sure and check your face; your mouth is disgusting and you don't want any food or toothpaste on your lips. I learned this lesson the hard way. One time, I had an interview and at the end of it I got in my car and though it went pretty well. Driving home, I was pretty confident I got the job, but just as I went to adjust my rear-view mirror I realized I had a red substance all over my face, and recalled that I had eaten pizza – a lot of it – for lunch, and the red stuff was pizza sauce. It could have been a lot worse I suppose. I licked it off and kept driving. Also, check your zipper.   It's common human decency to let someone know when they've got stuff on their face, and so it takes a cold son of a bitch to stare at you for forty-five minutes staring at your pizza-sauce covered face knowing that they're not going to hire you and let you make a fool of yourself, but it's the real world I suppose. The best interview I ever went on lasted about thirty seconds because they just told me the interview was over right away and didn't keep me waiting. I really appreciated that, and it freed up a few minutes for me to actually enjoy the company of the people sitting across from me asking me stupid questions.

Let's assume the interview went well, and you actually got a job (however unlikely this may be). Now that you've got yourself a job, the trick to keeping it is to look busy, especially when managers are around. Managers are people with no social skills that sit in a room upstairs and watch what you do on a camera. They never praise you, and if you're good at your job, they will actively work towards your demise. Their primary responsibilities include cutting your hours, telling you that you don't get a raise, so if you enjoy these activities or are a born douche bag, consider a career in management.

The Snooze Button

The Snooze Button was invented some time shortly after the invention of the alarm clock itself. I remember when I discovered the snooze button as a young boy. It was early in the morning, and my alarm clock was going off. I didn't want to get up so I wondered to myself if there was a way that I could silence the alarm for about nine minutes so that I could get just a few seconds more of rest. This would allow me just enough time to toss and turn for 8 and 1 / 2 minutes, and sleep for the remaining 30 seconds, before starting the cycle all over again.

On the night I discovered the snooze button, I had prayed for a snow day, but like usual received the opposite of what I had asked for. As a result, I was forced from my slumber on this cold western New York morning by my alarm clock, which began emitting a heinous noise at the pre-agreed upon time of precisely 6am, Eastern Standard

Time. I rolled over, turned on a light, and examined the device to see if there was a way I could make it temporarily stop beeping. I noticed a few buttons - there was an on and off switch, and a bigger button. Faced with a decision, I weighed my options. If I turned the alarm off I would likely go back to bed and definitely miss the bus, which would lead to more serious problems in the future. If I kept the switch toggled to "on", the clock would keep making noise, and cause me most likely to kill myself right there. The latter option was undesirable for a couple reasons; I feared that I would make my loved ones sad but, more importantly, it was Taco Tuesday at school and I wasn't going to miss that for anything. I was about to choose when, like a dove appearing from the heavens, I noticed that the biggest button on the whole clock read in capital letters SNOOZE, and I rejoiced thinking to myself "that's exactly what I want to do," and so I extended my index finger, and pecked the button one time. Magically, the noise ceased and I realized that from that moment on, my life would never be the same.

  This was the first time I had ever utilized the snooze button, but it sure wouldn't be the last. Over the next few months, the Snooze button grew on me like something that grows on something else, and has since claimed numerous hours of my life.

  When I first discovered the Snooze button, I was a little confused, mostly because I thought the alarm clock's purpose was to wake people up, not offer encouragement to go back to sleep. If I was in the market for a sleep aide, I would have simply struck up conversation with a woman, but my real issue lied in actually waking up in the morning.

At the time I didn't care about any of the ideology because I was too tired and just wanted to get back to sleep, and the Snooze button helped me do just that by returning the room to silent, thereby liberating me from the auditory oppression I had been experiencing and allowed me to curl up into a tight ball and thrust my thumb deep into my mouth.

My relationship with the alarm clock and best be described as "love-hate." Okay, more hate than love. At first, it was making a sound that was so offensive, and I resented it for that. But then, thanks to the snooze button, it would turn around and free me from the same noise, and I would forget about the abuse I had just endured. It was definitely like some sort of abusive relationship, and I didn't know whether to thank the clock or break it, and so I did neither.

No sooner after I regained my blissful state of unconsciousness, the stupid thing began going off again. This really tried my patience, and I wanted to snap. Only nine minutes had passed, and already the clock wanted to ruin my life again. I tried everything to ignore it. Well, two things: tuning it out, and covering my ears with my pillows, but the noise penetrated my soul and tried to possess it until, once more, I gave that little miracle button a firm poke. To my delight, the noise stopped, and I slipped back into bed before reassuming the fetal position. I drifted off real fast this time, and in an effort to escape the sound that would probably be returning as it had done already two times in the same morning, forgot about the clock quicker than the French forgot about America after D-day. All was peaceful for about exactly nine more minutes, at which point I was awoken again. This process continued for a total of 7 times, and caused me to go through menopause.

Clearly, the morning in question was off to a rough start, but the alarm clock wasn't the only thorn in my side attempting to not let me keep sleeping. There was also my mom, who for whatever reason had imposed "getting out of bed" #1 on my priority list. She had been coming in the room while the alarm clock was beeping because it had woken her up too and, irritated, she told me to "shut that damn thing off and get up." I told her I was trying, but she didn't understand.

Before I proceed any further, I should add a little backstory about my mom. She had come into the picture a few years prior when I was just an infant. I don't remember when, exactly, because my memory was barely functional when we first met, but I'm told by a few individuals that the day was June 6 during a year where nothing else of importance occured. The first time I saw her I tried squirming away, but she managed to corral me for several years, apparently by feeding and clothing me and by performing several other tasks that directly ensured my day-to-day survival. I grew fond of this mystery stranger, who seemed to have been sent by some other universe to care for me, and began calling her Mom. I'm not sure why I gave her that title, but my guess is that I heard some other kid calling their overlord by the same name, and so I did too.

During the morning when I found the Snooze button, Mom had been drifting in and out my room. She was reminding me in not so pleasant terms that I should wake up, and she made it pretty clear that the deadline for doing so was now, and she didn't hesitate to use ruthless tactics waking me up. For instance, she said that I would miss the bus for school and become a failure, and turned the light on in my room to deter falling back asleep. She also left the door to my room open, and I'm convinced purposely went into the bathroom that was next to my room and made excessive noise. And she attempted repeatedly to engage me in polite conversation. Not wanting any of it, I tried reasoning with her, and begged for just "five more minutes" – anything that could lead to more sleep. I wondered silently if she, too, might have a Snooze button somewhere on her that I could push, but there was nothing I could do. She wasn't going to back down, and she was bigger than me.

Mommy allowed the charade of the alarm clock sounding, me hitting the snooze button, her telling me to get up, and me going back to sleep for about seven Snooze rotations. Throughout the course of that hour, something must have pushed her over the edge, because, in between one of my nine minute siestas, I felt a cold liquid run all over my upper-body. I awoke to see her moving swiftly towards the exit of my room with a cup in her hand, angrily commanding me yet again to "get up now!" More confused than the Toronto mayor in a drunken stupor, I rolled over in my bed and discovered next to me a small collection of ice cubes lying in a puddle of some mysterious liquid. I ran a series of tests, and concluded that the liquid it was water, and discerned that that the ice had been added on purpose in order to make the water a colder temperature than the ground would otherwise have it be. Mom's decision to pour water on me was an attack both on my consciousness, and my physical well-being; as you know, hypothermia is very serious and I was headed in that direction fast. Indeed, she had found my Kryptonite/Achilles heel/major weakness, a mixture of ice and water, or "ice water," as it's referred to on the street. Her ingenious concoction was successful for several reasons, the most notable being that I don't like being cold, or tired, or awake, and now I was all three of these things at once. Frankly, it was a miracle I survived. I can handle being wet; in fact, I had spent several New Years Eves in a hot tub, and found it refreshing, but being wet and cold at the same time was a different story, and so I was stuck in between a rock and a hard place, so to speak. I was convinced that no snooze button in the world could erase the misery I was experiencing. Well, maybe the blow dryer could have helped, but mom was using it at the time, and I had burned my skin with one previously, so I ruled that out. I began weeping, and clicked the alarm clock from on to off and proceeded to the bathroom.

Crying, I turned on the water. I made a point to turn on the middle knob before entering the shower in order to let the water heat up because I did not want to endure, as I had in the past, the shock from that first burst of water when it comes from the shower head that is, for some inexplicable reason, always cold. Well, probably the reason it is always cold at first is because the water molecules that stay in the pipes in between shower usages do not get to hang out near the water-heater like the other molecules, as they all await their destiny in a sewer somewhere.

With the hot water pouring over me, my problems seemed to melt away, and I once again forgot about the multiple run-ins with Snooze button that had caused me so much pain just moments before. This newfound warmth and comfort was short-lived, due to the arrival of the school bus now reaching serious imminence, and because when I turned off the water and whipped open the bathroom curtain, was greeted by air that must have been colder than it was on the night of April 15, 1912, the night of the sinking of the unsinkable ship, Titanic which took the life of the young Jack Dawson, who had recently fallen in love with a certain Rose something or other.

At some point during my never-ending struggle with waking up, I acquired another alarm clock to help, complete with Snooze button, and so now there are two Snooze buttons in my room. It's most unfortunate that things had to get to this point, but when faced with waking up in the morning and not waking up, I find that the alarm clock really is effective.

For better or worse, the Snooze button came into existence, and has ruined countless lives, but it's here now and so I better learn how to cope with it, much like the atomic bomb. I thought the inventor of the atomic bomb, Robert Oppenheimer, was referring to the invention of the Snooze button when he said "We knew the world would not be the same. A few people laughed, a few people cried, most people were silent. I remembered the line from the Hindu scripture, the Bhagavad-Gita... "Now, I am become Death, the destroyer of worlds" but I was wrong – he wasn't talking about the Snooze button at all. Oops…my bad, aside from WMD, it's creation has been the most destructive force ever invented in the history of the world for several reasons – none of which I feel like elaborating upon now, and its usage should be approached with extreme caution. After all, nobody wants to be late for work. I have appropriately named my alarm clocks Hiroshima and Nagasaki as an ever-present reminder of its impact on the world, and continue to pray for a Snooze-buttonless world.

Insurance is Evil

State farm is not a good neighbor, that's false advertising. They're not even a neighbor at all. It's some place you call and send money when you have your car registered so that when you get pulled over you can tell the cop you have insurance. I've never had a neighbor come over four times a year asking for three hundred dollars in exchange for 70 pages of gibberish. Good...

Getting Accepted Into School

I finally got into school. Three of them at the same time, in fact, after being rejected several times from many others for various reasons, mostly due to my many deficiencies and character flaws. The University at Toledo told me I didn't fit in with their MBA culture, to which I responded "why, because I'm not from India?" then I pointed out that the director was male and his entire staff was female, and that probably it was a combination of a few things like that which led to my exclusion from the program. To validate my theory, consider that the school changed their facebook profile picture of Charlie and the 15 angels less than a week later, and fixed the broken treadmills in the gym, about which I also sent a disgruntled e-mail.

I'm glad I didn't get in there, because I looked at someone's financial homework the other day and I couldn't think of anything I'd rather do less than stare at a bunch of numbers all day. Worse, I'd still be in Buffalo…erm… Toledo. When I was your age, it was pretty simple, you either had a dollar or you didn't, and there was no need for financial analysis. Oh well, I guess that's one way to create jobs.

But yes, I got into school. And it felt good. So good, in fact, that I ordered a mimosa the next day. And another mimosa, and then went to some kids' party and jumped around in the bounce-house and when I was leaving I popped the bounce house so none of the kids could play in it. Then the kids started crying and I laughed because it was funny. But it also got me thinking and imagining things a la "I have a dream" by Martin Luther King, like how far I could dropkick a kid? I can punt a football at least 40 yards, which is pretty good I think, but I feel like if I punted a child, or even a toddler, he or she wouldn't even go 10 yards even if they happened to weigh the same as a football. This probably has something to do with physics. Who knows, I don't like physics but I do know the basic two laws: everything has an equal or opposite reaction, and Mike the Situation is, without a doubt, gay. That's pretty much all there is to know about physics.

The best part about getting into school was that my friend actually bought me a cake with the school's colors which, incidentally, were the same colors as those of the tri-town Trojans pee-wee football team in the rural expanse of land where I was spawned and spent a good chunk of most of my life before taking a plane to England and meeting my soulmate on OK Cupid at age 69 as part of a study abroad program.

The Trojan's colors were, green and gold, but this was before they disbanded before rebanding for what I presume was a boring reason. Needless to say, we were confused when we saw trojan commercials on TV with our football team nowhere to be found.

Side joke:

Q: What's worse than naming your football team after contraception?

A: Letting Danica Patrick behind the wheel of your car. Seriously, the DWI threshold for her should be 0.00.

It was about the time the Trojans won the pee wee championship that my best friend impregnated his girlfriend on a dare and got his first DWI, which we celebrated by rearranging the neighbor's Christmas ornamental reindeer into more interesting positions, and taking some selfies. Coincidentally, it was my 10th birthday so we had actually killed two birds with one stone, plus about 10 more birds because I was also learning how to hunt at that age and needed something to practice on, not in the traditional sense, but in a more deranged and disturbing way. To answer your question, yes those videos glorifying violence do effect children.

Everything was going great until the american psychological association declared selfitis (the act of taking selfies) an actual disease, and I'm glad it did but I read one time in the Romance of the Rose by Guillaume de Lorris about Narcissism, and concluded that the selfie disorder and narcissism are one in the same thing. By the way, do you know how much it costs to operate a mental ward per person? About $10,000 a person for a 10 day all-expenses paid visit, courtesy of the taxpayer-funded Medicaid program. And this includes guaranteed access to experimental drugs that cause you to grow man boobs. It's all good though, because if you did happen to eat a bunch of Risperdal and grow the boobs, you're now able to file a lawsuit by calling a 1-800 number; I saw it in a TV commercial and that's how I know it's true. Thanks a lot, Freud – your book is going in the same pile where I put my copy of Mein Kampf by Hiter…

Right, so basically I applied to the school on-line, and went back and forth with the admissions counselor for what seemed like an eternity. She was in no way, shape, or form, interested in meeting me halfway so, as I've learned in life, I was going to have to do all the work. I went over to her office and we discussed the details of the arrangement – I would register for classes, and she would, and I quote, "allow me to do so." I wasn't exactly the best candidate for the position, I guess, because she requested that I wear a mask next time of a famous football player that she was in love with because it would greatly improve the likelihood of my getting into the school, and would expedite the process. I obliged, and soon thereafter I was sitting in her office paranoid and wearing a Michael Vick mask, crossing my fingers because that means something.

I was wrong in the end though. The admissions counselor, Elaine, went above and beyond to help me navigate the academic bureaucracy, did a great job, and I'll be sure and save her a piece of cake

A Short Argument in Favor of Kids

I would like to have a kid so he could do stuff for me, like scratch my back and get me food. The problem with having a kid is that you pretty much have to wait until it's about three before you can use it. You'll want to keep in mind, too, that it's also about this age that the woman you married in order to have the kid will start divorcing you, if she hasn't already. I wouldn't be discouraged by this. Just be prepared to buy a few business suits to impress the judge during your custody battle. In case you're wondering, yes, you want the kid. Why? Because now you're single and ready to mingle and you've got an ace up your sleeve when it comes to finding Mrs. Right #2, AKA the perfect little wingman. A puppy-kid combo is a double whammy when it comes to flirting. If you don't have a small dog, borrow one from your neighbor. Keep in mind that kids are only cute for about ten years, so start looking for work out-of-state around age nine so you have a reason to leave, and plenty of time to move and start your new job comfortably. This is imperative because not only will a teenager cramp your dating life, you will successfully avoid those awkward talk about birds and bees and other unspeakable. Of course this wouldn't be an issue of kids could be neutered and, unfortunately, they can't. Lather, rinse, repeat.

Animals

Cows

When I drive by cows I start salivating, which means that to the best of my knowledge, the cow is the only animal that looks delicious while it's still alive. Sometimes when I drive down the road and I see a cow grazing in the field, I stop and lick my lips. Oddly enough, he's usually licking his too. Cows have massive tongues, just like Miley Cyrus. Believe it or not, they have quite a few things in common with her. Like Miley, they're not very smart, and they spend most of the day grazing in the pasture, eating grass, and rocking out stages all over the USA. Humans should figure out how to eat grass too, not to solve the hunger epidemic, or as a substitute for mowing the lawn, but just because it would be neat if we could eat grass.

Cows are good for a lot of other reasons, and we would do well to learn from them. For instance, most cows are black and white, which means there is no issue when it comes to racial inequality. Maybe to alleviate racial tensions among humans, white people could paint black spots on themselves and vice-versa. There are also brown cows, though. It would be a lot of work to paint them so maybe we could build a huge fence in order to keep them from digging under, climbing over, or sneaking across in vans to be with the other cows, if you catch my drift. If you don't catch my drift, I'm talking about Mexicans. Lo ciento, amigos.

Sometimes cows get a bad rap, and it must be insulting to them. One time, someone called this guy's mom a "fat cow" and he got really upset. I was confused because I figured it would be a compliment, because cows are great. He was mad, so I was like, "no dude, your mom's a fat cow. Don't you get it? That mean she's awesome"… no shame in that! He assaulted me shortly thereafter, and I don't know why; I think he was retarded or something.

Another reason cows are so awesome is because they produce milk, one of the greatest beverages on the planet. In this regard, I feel like we got screwed over by mother nature when it comes to "teets." What I mean by that is I only have two "teets," and they are basically useless. Maybe if I was a female, this wouldn't be the case. On the other hand, cows have four big teets that produce all sorts of milk, including but not limited to 1%, 2%, Whole Milk, Vitamin D, non-fat, and most importantly, chocolate. For some reason, the government is so scared of milk, that it limits how much it can be sold for. I bet this makes the cows feel dirty and used. Probably not as dirty and used as they must feel just before that bullet goes through their head when they're big enough and worth it to be eaten, but used nonetheless. If I were cows, I would consider banning together and doing something about this injustice. But, given that they are capable of practically nothing, I understand how unrealistic this might be.

I bet one of the worst parts about being a cow is they never get to taste the fruits of their labor, so to speak. No cow has ever drank its own milk. It's a tragic sort of irony in a way, I think. It's like those little kids in China who work barefoot all day as interns in a shoe factory.

We all know that cows are an excellent source of Calcium, but did you know that they are also an excellent source of entertainment? For instance, before TV, there was cow-tipping. This is when cows just stand there at night, meditating or something, and while they're doing it you walk up and push them over, ideally breaking their ribs so they can't get up. It's supposed to be pretty funny, but I don't actually know because I've never done it, I just saw it on TV one time; it might be a myth.

The only downside to cows is the fact that they're slow. They barely move. This makes it incredibly difficult to taunt them, or get them to do anything. You can say "come here" or "go over there" and they just stand there and stare at you. Occasionally, if you irritate them enough when you're standing behind them, they will try and kick you. But that's about all the action you're going to get from a cow, so don't expect much when it comes to movement.

Dogs

If were a dog, I would bark for most of the day, especially in the mornings on weekends so that I could wake everyone up. On those days I would start around 3am and go until 11 or so, just to make sure I got the attention of everyone. Then when they got mad I would just wag my tail like nothing happened and "be the bigger dog," so to speak. My barking would protect people from real threats like wind and kids on bicycles.

I wouldn't want to be just any dog. My owners would need to have a ton of money, and I wouldn't want to be neglected or owned by Michael Vick. A major reason I want to be a dog is so that I could visit the doctor. In an age of not being able to go to the doctor because insurance companies are a ponzi scheme, this would be a dream come true. I know it would just be a veterinarian but that would be better than seeing my roommate, who, if forced to choose, I would list as my current medical provider even though his only medical qualifications include CPR and a Lifeguard Certification. This would be fine if I was drowning or almost dead on the floor not breathing, but most of the time I just need someone to give me my shots and tell me to exercise more. Actually, if I was a dog he wouldn't even need to remind me to exercise, because I would constantly be going on walks and, for some reason, would find them enjoyable. If I happened to end up being a greyhound, I'd probably enter into a lot of road races with other dogs and win medals and t-shirts; who knows, maybe make a living at it and retire early.

My favorite part about walks would be the pooping because nowhere else in the world do you have the freedom to take a huge s**t in a stranger's backyard with someone waiting behind you with a plastic bag to scoop it up, Nor would I have any shame in doing it in front of anyone and everyone, just as God intended. Another perk of being a dog is that you get a comfortable bed. A lot of dogs I know even have their own private doghouse, which would be awesome.

As a dog, I would pretty much be able to get away with anything, and would take full advantage of this. I know this because one time when I was younger I saw this kid get bit by a dog and the owners of the dog didn't even kill it! With this in mind, the first person on my to-bite list would be the postman, of course. It's like the rite of passage for dogs, and I would do my best to grab that blue bastard by the arm and shake until all of the mail in his hands was on the ground. Then I would pick up the mail and take it to my owners and get a treat. There would be no better way to start a day. Other popular targets would include people on bicycles and runners. I don't know what it is about those cyclists and runners but, whenever I saw one, I would instantly start chasing them and, ideally, bite them too. If that's not an option, chasing is still fun, and if you're good at it, you can still achieve desirable results. For instance, you can scare the runner into oncoming traffic or get them to crash their bike going 50mph downhill. Then, you just sit back and enjoy the fruits of your labor – watching them plow into oncoming traffic or fall into a ditch. Maybe even bite them again while they're on the ground for good measure.

Afterwards, you just go about your business and if the person does defend themselves, your owner will defiantly stick up for you. And then you've got him working on the problem so you can get back to more important things, like sniffing bushes.

RIP to my dog Butches, 1996 – 2007

Gorillas

The gorilla is probably the most popular animal in the zoo, and understandably so. He looks like a human (sort of), moves like a human, and takes care of his children like a human. It's pretty adorable. When sitting in front of the gorilla exhibit, your mind inevitably begins to wander, and you meditate on just where it is our species come from. At about that moment, one of the more agitated gorillas slams the clear wall where a kid is standing and taunting him and, you think to yourself, "I really wish that wall hadn't been there because that would have been funny. " Later on in your trip to the zoo, you wish the same thing for the fence in between the lion and zebra exhibit. I, for one, would like to see a little more action in my trips to the zoo. Alas, we haven't evolved quite yet to that point as a species.

We feel a certain kinship to the apes. The dad sits stoically high up on a branch and monitors the family, while the mother plays and nurses her in the hammock. You've got a few cousins or orphans running around too, swinging from vine to vine and messing around with each other, and it makes you think you're a much better tree-climber than you actually are. You get the sense that the gorillas know they are being watched, and it makes you feel sad for them. You probably shouldn't, because it takes two to gawk and it may very well be that the joke is on us. What I mean is that, given the fact that I need to travel to a metropolitan area to watch nature behind a glass cage may be an indication that our species took a wrong turn somewhere. Indeed, we took a lot of right ones when you consider electricity and whatnot, but it's sad – and not for the gorillas – that our relationship with nature has become day trip to the zoo.

You're pretty content at this point sitting in front of the exhibit and watching them do their thing, and then everything changes the moment your eye notices one of them sitting in the corner, devouring his own feces. You begin to think to yourself that perhaps we never evolved from these things after all, and that maybe this was all a mistake; you want to escape your past, and you feel deep shame when you disgustingly begin to wonder what, in fact, your own poop tastes like. But it will end there, because you won't dare try it for fear that one day you'll have to play "never have I ever" and subsequently take a drink when someone finishes their statement with "eaten my own poop." If this ever happens, you're better off registering as a sex offender.

Now you're completely done with the gorilla exhibit and you decide to move on. You linger a little longer and watch him in disgust and judgment as he continues doing the unthinkable, and just when you're about leave him behind forever, things go from bad to worse… another smaller gorilla comes along and attempts to steal some of his poop dinner. You think that probably the big gorilla is just going to let it go but, no, he pushes him away and boldly declares that he should find his own. You want to tell the little gorilla to simply take a dump and then he'll have that, but it's 5:30 and you've got to hurry up and see the rest of the exhibits before the zoo closes at 7. You approach the gorilla exhibit with caution from that point on, as you have become made aware of their capabilities.

Squirrels

Squirrels are my favorite rodent. They're like rats, but their faces are tolerable to look at, and they've got that nice bushy tale and usually carry around an acorn. How could you not like squirrels? Squirrels, however, don't respect humans. I'm pretty used to being disrespected, but I figure I need to draw the line somewhere, and that line is squirrels. In DC the squirrels barely move over when you walk by them, and they're constantly staring at you. That's rude. It's fun to watch them dig holes all day, plant their acorns, and then cover them up for, apparently, no reason. I don't recall ever having seen a squirrel return to his acorn to dig it up and eat it. Now that I think about it, I don't recall caring about that either. Squirrels are everywhere and, for me personally, seeing them generally makes my life better. Animals that aren't a threat to us tend to have that effect, I think. One thing that annoys me about them is that they won't let you pick them up. They'll run out in front your car while you're doing 50mph, so it's kind of stupid that they won't just let me pick them up, since you never really hear about people doing mean things to them.

In fact, since I occasionally feed them, the right thing for the squirrel to do, I think, would be to let me handle him for a few minutes should I wish.

It has long been on my bucket list to catch a squirrel with my bare hands, and the other day, I had a good networking opportunity to do just that while walking through a parking lot. I noticed a squirrel perched up on a garbage can with his head down in the trash looking for stuff. I assume he was looking for sweets or something because there were acorns all over the parking lot – he could have just went after those. So he was pretty focused. And so was I. I walked right over to him and got within in striking distance, but just before I went to grab him, realized that I was wearing a suit and tie and that this was, at least for me, an expensive purchase. I also remembered that until this point in time, I had never caught a squirrel with my bare hands in the past, nor had this particularly squirrel been picked up by a human before, so it would be a new experience for both of us. I ascertained that he would probably not like being held and that there was a good chance he would instinctively begin gnawing ferociously at my hand and likely give me rabies or, worse, get blood on my good clothes. Hey, it's 2013, and unless I walk around looking good, I won't be able to have a job that allows me to continue to not carry health insurance on myself. It's complicated, I know. Sidebar: wouldn't it be great if our moronic race went after insurance companies themselves – the real scam artists – and not the American public? Nah, you're right let's keep pretending this is a joke.

Anyway, instead of catching the little guy, I decided just to stomp my foot like an asshole and scare him. Sure enough, it was a lot of fun, for me at least. He shot me an angry glare, then ran away from the garbage to safe distance at which point he stopped again and fluffed his tale like an idiot, as if to let me know that I had better watch my back now.

I could sense that I had pissed off not only this squirrel, but his clan, or whatever you call a pack of squirrels too because, as I walked away I could sense the presence of more than one irritated squirrel. I looked to my right, and there was one there, also fluffing his tail, in what I'm convinced was an attempt to communicate with the other squirrels on their plan of attack should I decide to keep getting involved with their affairs. I turned around quickly, and there were a couple others there tool fidgeting around kind of inconspicuously. Leaving, I returned to my perch three floors up and observed as they got back to work diligently digging, planting, and covering up. In conclusion, I might sprinkle a little salt on their nuts for them tomorrow because they must be sick of eating those bland ones. I know I would be, and I know my nuts always taste better salty.

Skunks

The skunk is a logical follow-up to the squirrel because it doesn't have any respect for people either – nor should it. We humans have no choice but to bow to the skunk every time we see it and this is because most of us have never been sprayed by a skunk and we would like to keep it that way. There's probably a statistic out there somewhere indicating how one in five people know someone who has been sprayed by a skunk. I don't know anyone who has, but I recall hearing once about someone who had a dog that got sprayed by a skunk, and I remember this because that person probably talked about that occurrence for a good forty-five minutes. It's not their fault I let them talk about their dog for that long, it's mine for not changing the subject. Lesson learned.

The skunk definitely has no friends, which I can relate to, and so it gets a little pity from me there. But for the most part, I don't feel bad for the creature because when you walk around insisting that everything else smell like five hundred tons of ass, you pretty much get what you deserve. All the skunk does is strut around lethargically looking for God-knows-what. Seriously, what do these things even eat? I don't know because all I can think about when I see one is "this stupid thing better not come near me." Unfortunately for the skunk, it has approximately zero redeeming qualities. And I say that this is an approximation because it does look like Dale Earnhardt's car and the Oakland Raiders, which is pretty cool, but were it not for that, the skunk would lean a 100% bane of an existence.

On two occasions, my life has been ruined by skunks, and I won't ever forgive them for it. I take that back; I may forgive, but I certainly won't forget. On the first such instance, I was riding my bicycle home at dusk on a paved bike path through the woods. It was almost pitch black, and I was fairly close to home when I looked up ahead and, sure as hell, there was a skunk ambling along the path. You've heard the phrase "never bring a knife to a gun fight" and, keeping this in mind, I didn't have anything on me that I could spray on him to make him smell worse than he would have made me smell, if you know what I mean, and so I was forced to retreat. This caused me great stress because it was getting late and I had been busy being distracted so it was much later than I wanted to get home, and now I had to find another route home, kinda like that one time Columbus was looking for an alternate route to India but wound up in Haiti and everyone told us he landed in Virginia or something and the Minnesota Vikings were all there. Hey don't ask me, I was too busy trying to make the teacher cry to pay attention in history class (hey, I'm sorry and you were right, I should have paid attention). Oh well, doesn't do any good living in the past. Anyway, I turned around and he continued zigzagging across the path like an asshole. The second time a skunk ruined my life was pretty much the same as the first except the skunk(s) (there were two this time) were milling about the front of my apartment door while I was heading out for work doing what skunks do best: NOTHING, and, pissing me off. As a result I was late. Someone told me that I should have just went for it and that they wouldn't have bothered me. Yeah, okay buddy, I thought… get bent. In short, skunks are probably the only animal that, if you heard they were going to be extinct soon, you would rejoice and wonder how you could contribute to making that happen even quicker. I know I would.